WITHDRAWN

Staying Safe Online

By SHANNON MCCLINTOCK MILLER

Illustrations by KATHRYN DURST

Music by EMILY ARROW

CANTATA
LEARNING

WWW.CANTATALEARNING.COM

CANTATA
LEARNING

Published by Cantata Learning
1710 Roe Crest Drive
North Mankato, MN 56003
www.cantatalearning.com

Library of Congress Cataloging-in-Publication Data
Names: Miller, Shannon (Shannon McClintock), author. | Durst, Kathryn,
 illustrator. | Arrow, Emily, composer.
Title: Staying safe online / by Shannon McClintock Miller ; illustrations by
 Kathryn Durst ; music by Emily Arrow.
Description: North Mankato, MN : Cantata Learning, [2018] | Series: Library
 skills | Includes bibliographical references.
Identifiers: LCCN 2017007561 (print) | LCCN 2017017932 (ebook) | ISBN
 9781684100507 | ISBN 9781684100491 (hardcover : alk. paper)
Subjects: LCSH: Internet and children--Juvenile literature. |
 Internet--Safety measures--Juvenile literature. | Internet--Songs and
 music. | Children's songs, English--United States--Texts.
Classification: LCC HQ784.I58 (ebook) | LCC HQ784.I58 M556 2018 (print) | DDC
 004.67/8083--dc23
LC record available at https://lccn.loc.gov/2017007561

Book design, Tim Palin Creative
Editorial direction, Flat Sole Studio
Executive musical production and direction, Elizabeth Draper
Music arranged and produced by Emily Arrow

Printed in the United States of America in North Mankato, Minnesota.
072017 0367CGF17

ACCESS THE MUSIC!
SCAN CODE WITH MOBILE APP
CANTATALEARNING.COM

TIPS TO SUPPORT LITERACY AT HOME

WHY READING AND SINGING WITH YOUR CHILD IS SO IMPORTANT

Daily reading with your child leads to increased academic achievement. Music and songs, specifically rhyming songs, are a fun and easy way to build early literacy and language development. Music skills correlate significantly with both phonological awareness and reading development. Singing helps build vocabulary and speech development. And reading and appreciating music together is a wonderful way to strengthen your relationship.

READ AND SING EVERY DAY!

TIPS FOR USING CANTATA LEARNING BOOKS AND SONGS DURING YOUR DAILY STORY TIME

1. As you sing and read, point out the different words on the page that rhyme. Suggest other words that rhyme.

2. Memorize simple rhymes such as Itsy Bitsy Spider and sing them together. This encourages comprehension skills and early literacy skills.

3. Use the questions in the back of each book to guide your singing and storytelling.

4. Read the included sheet music with your child while you listen to the song. How do the music notes correlate to the words of the song?

5. Sing along on the go and at home. Access music by scanning the QR code on each Cantata book. You can also stream or download the music for free to your computer, smartphone, or mobile device.

Devoting time to daily reading shows that you are available for your child. Together, you are building language, literacy, and listening skills.

Have fun reading and singing!

Going online is a lot of fun. There are games to play, videos to watch, and **endless** things to learn. But not every site is safe for you to visit. Ask a trusted adult about safety rules for when you are online.

Now turn the page to learn about staying safe online. Remember to sing along!

COMPUTER STATION

5

Stay safe online by being smart.
Think with your head and with your heart.

Think with your heart. Stay safe online.
Don't share too much. Only **post** what's kind.

Your name, your age, or where you live is not **info** that you should give.

Keep special dates, and **passwords** too, as secrets that are just for you.

The online world is really large.
Your grown-ups help you stay in charge.

Beware of strangers you don't know.
If something's not right, tell a grown-up so.

Stay safe online by being smart.
Think with your head and with your heart.

Think with your heart. Stay safe online.
Don't share too much. Only post what's kind.

Check out sites that your grown-ups okay.
Ask an adult if it's safe to play!

Games are great for learning too.
Make sure they are right for you.

It's always okay to ask for help.
That's how we learn to help ourselves!

Technology is fun, it's true!
And staying safe is up to you.

Stay safe online by being smart.
Think with your head and with your heart.

Think with your heart. Stay safe online.
Don't share too much. Only post what's kind.

Stay safe online by being smart.
Think with your head and with your heart.

Think with your heart. Stay safe online.
Don't share too much. Only post what's kind.

SONG LYRICS
Staying Safe Online

Stay safe online by being smart.
Think with your head and with your heart.
Think with your heart. Stay safe online.
Don't share too much. Only post what's kind.

Your name, your age, or where you live
is not info that you should give.
Keep special dates, and passwords too,
as secrets that are just for you.

The online world is really large.
Your grown-ups help you stay in charge.
Beware of strangers you don't know.
If something's not right, tell a grown-up so.

Stay safe online by being smart.
Think with your head and with your heart.
Think with your heart. Stay safe online.
Don't share too much. Only post what's kind.

Check out sites that your grown-ups okay.
Ask an adult if it's safe to play!
Games are great for learning too.
Make sure they are right for you.

It's always okay to ask for help.
That's how we learn to help ourselves!
Technology is fun. It's true!
And staying safe is up to you.

Stay safe online by being smart.
Think with your head and with your heart.
Think with your heart. Stay safe online.
Don't share too much. Only post what's kind.

Stay safe online by being smart.
Think with your head and with your heart.
Think with your heart. Stay safe online.
Don't share too much. Only post what's kind.

Staying Safe Online

Kindie
Emily Arrow

Chorus

Stay safe on-line by be-ing smart. Think with your head and with your heart.

Think with your heart. Stay safe on-line. Don't share too much. On-ly post what's kind.

Verse

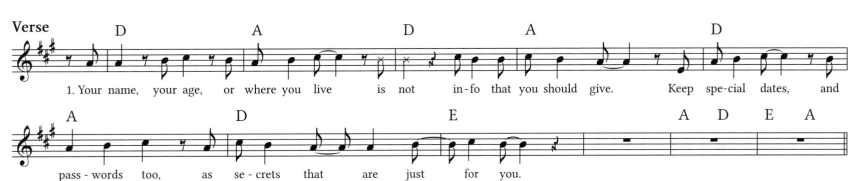

1. Your name, your age, or where you live is not in-fo that you should give. Keep spe-cial dates, and

pass-words too, as se-crets that are just for you.

Verse 2
The online world is really large.
Your grown-ups help you stay in charge.
Beware of strangers you don't know.
If something's not right, tell a grown-up so.

Chorus

Verse 3
Check out sites that your grown-ups okay.
Ask an adult if it's safe to play!
Games are great for learning too.
Make sure they are right for you.

Verse 4
It's always okay to ask for help.
That's how we learn to help ourselves!
Technology is fun. It's true!
And staying safe is up to you.

Chorus (x2)

GLOSSARY

endless—having no end

info—short for information

passwords—letters and numbers that allow you to use a computer or website

post—to put something online

technology—any device that solves a problem

GUIDED READING ACTIVITIES

1. What do you like to do online? What rules do you follow to keep yourself safe while online?

2. Adults have rules to keep us safe. What rules keep you safe at home? What rules keep you safe at school?

3. Imagine that you're making a website all about you. What would you put on your website? Now draw a picture of what your website would look like!

TO LEARN MORE

Jennings, Rosemary. *Safe Online*. New York: Powerkids Press, 2017.

Lee, Sally. *Staying Safe Online*. North Mankato, MN: Capstone, 2012.

Mcaneney, Caitie. *Online Safety*. New York: Powerkids Press, 2015.

Rustad, Martha E. H. *Learning About Privacy*. North Mankato, MN: Capstone, 2015.